W9-CPN-044

Money

Money and Me

Money

by
Amy Adelstein

Rourke Publications, Inc.
Vero Beach, FL 32964

Photo on page 2 by Jim Whitmer.

Produced by Salem Press, Inc.

Copyright © 1997, by Rourke Publications, Inc.
All rights in this book are reserved. No part of this work may be used or reproduced in any manner whatsoever or transmitted in any form or by any means, electronic or mechanical, including photocopy, recording, or any information storage and retrieval system, without written permission from the copyright owner except in the case of brief quotations embodied in critical articles and reviews. For information address the publisher, Rourke Publications, Inc., P.O. Box 3328, Vero Beach, Florida 32964.

∞ The paper used in these volumes conforms to the American National Standard for Permanence of Paper for Printed Library Materials, Z39.48-1984.

Library of Congress Cataloging-in-Publication Data
Adelstein, Amy, 1956-
   Money / by Amy Adelstein.
      p.   cm. — (Money and me)
   Includes bibliographical references and index.
   Summary: Discusses what money is, where to get it, its rules, the advantages of having it, and how cash, checks, and credit cards differ.
   ISBN 0-86625-611-3
   1. Money—Juvenile literature. 2. Finance, Personal—Juvenile literature. [1. Money. 2. Finance, Personal.] I. Title. II. Series.
HG221.5.A32   1997
332.4—dc21   97-6365
                                                                         CIP
                                                                          AC

First Printing

PRINTED IN THE UNITED STATES OF AMERICA

Contents

What Is It?

You and your brother are home after trick-or-treating. You look over your treats and find three chocolate bars with nuts. You don't like nuts, but your brother likes them very much. "What will you give me for the chocolate bars?" you ask him.

"This box of chocolate-covered raisins," he answers.

"That's not enough. Give me that box of plain raisins, too. Then we have a deal," you say. Your brother agrees.

Barter and Exchange

You and your brother have traded things you have for things you want. You have bartered. Bartering is the simplest way of swapping, or exchanging, things.

What if your brother didn't have any treats you wanted? What would you do? Is there something you both think is valuable? Maybe you both collect baseball cards. A baseball card could be your *medium of exchange*. It could allow you and your brother to trade what you have for what you want.

Your brother could give you money for the chocolate bars instead. Money lets us exchange

things easily. We all agree it has value. Money is marked with words and numbers that indicate its value. You can read the words "five dollars" on a five-dollar bill. You can also read "five cents" on a nickel. The value you read on money is its *face value*. The face value tells you how much of something you can buy with that money.

Sometimes, the face value is a lot more than the money itself is worth. For example, the paper and ink that make up a fifty-dollar bill don't cost fifty dollars. People agree, though, that the fifty-dollar bill can buy something that costs fifty dollars. You can also use a crumpled old bill to buy the same amount of things you can with a crisp new bill. The face value of the bill is what matters.

Types of Payment

When someone pays for something with coins or bills or a combination of both, they are using

Children enjoy exchanging or trading sports cards found in packs of bubble gum.
(James L. Shaffer)

Grocery shopping is an everyday activity that allows people to use different forms of payment. (James L. Shaffer)

cash. You have probably seen someone, maybe your grandmother, paying for groceries with cash.

Grandmother also could pay for the groceries with a *check.* The check has information on it that allows Grandmother to use it as money. Most important is Grandmother's signature on the check. The store can exchange Grandmother's signed check for money.

Grandmother also could use a *point-of-sale* (POS) debit card. This is a small plastic card. It takes money directly from Grandmother's bank account to pay for the groceries.

Your grandmother has still another way to buy groceries. She can use another type of plastic card called a *credit card.* She won't have to pay for the groceries right away. She can wait to pay until she receives a *bill.* The bill won't come from the store. It will come from the bank or company whose name is on the card. She may need to pay more than the price of the groceries. It all depends on when she pays the bill and how much of it she pays. When Grandmother uses her credit card, she pays on credit. That means she has time to pay. It also means someone trusts her to pay.

Types of Currency

Grandmother might use her credit card to buy something in another country. She probably couldn't use American dollars and cents. Every country has its own coins and bills, or *currency*. For example, Mexico has pesos and centavos. Nigeria has nairas and kobos. Thailand has bahts and satangs. Grandmother would have to buy the currency of the country she was visiting. The price of the currency is called its *rate of exchange*. This rate can change from day to day. Newspapers and banks often post information about exchange rates for different types of world currency. This information is useful for businesspeople and tourists who travel abroad.

A tourist in Caracas, Venezuela, consults a sign listing exchange rates for converting foreign currency into Venezuelan bolivars. (AP/Wide World Photos)

The price of a country's currency depends on its economic health. If the country's economic health is good, the price of its money goes up. If the country's economic health is bad, the price of its money goes down. The buying power of money depends on the strength of the country that issues it.

At one time, the value of money depended on its link to precious metals. People made coins out of precious metals like gold. People also could exchange paper currency for gold. The gold standard says that a government must back up its paper money with gold. During the 1930's, the United States stopped making gold coins. It also stopped exchanging bills for gold. It went off the gold standard. Other countries eventually did, too.

People use money with confidence it will buy something. On every U.S. bill is the treasury seal. This seal is the government's "seal of approval." It shows that the bill is *legal tender*. The government says people must accept these bills as payment. That is the law.

What Does Money Look Like?

U.S. bills also have drawings on them. The drawings on a five-dollar bill are different from those on a ten-dollar bill or a fifty-dollar bill. Every *denomination*, or money-amount bill, has its own drawings. The front of the bill has a picture of a famous person, such as Abraham Lincoln or Benjamin Franklin. The back usually has a picture of a building. These people and buildings are important to the history and government of the United States. Most of the people were presidents. The buildings are in the nation's current capital, Washington, D.C., or in its first capital, Philadelphia.

Denominations of U.S. coins also have pictures of people and things that our country

Type of Coin	Value	Color	Front Image	Back Image
Penny	$0.01	Copper	Abraham Lincoln	Lincoln Memorial in Washington, D.C.
Nickel	$0.05	Silver	Thomas Jefferson	Monticello, near Charlottesville, Va.
Dime	$0.10	Silver	Franklin D. Roosevelt	Torch with olive branch and oak branch
Quarter	$0.25	Silver	George Washington	American eagle with spreading wings
Half dollar	$0.50	Silver	John F. Kennedy	Great Seal of the United States
Dollar	$1.00	Silver	Dwight D. Eisenhower	Bald eagle holding an olive branch

values. We value them and we also value the money that bears their pictures. In 1979, the U.S. government issued a new one-dollar coin to honor a famous American woman. The coin had a picture of Susan B. Anthony, an early leader in the fight for women's rights. Some people did not like using the new coin because it was almost the same size as a quarter. Banks and businesses had trouble telling the difference between quarters and the new dollar coins. When demand for the coin fell off, the government decided to stop minting the Susan B. Anthony coin.

Collecting Coins

Some people collect special coins. Coin collectors value coins from certain years. They may collect dimes and quarters from before 1964, for example. These coins are made all of silver. Starting in the 1960's, the world had a shortage of silver. By 1970, dimes and quarters no longer contained any silver. Decades later, silver dimes and quarters are worth more than their face value.

The likeness of suffrage leader Susan B. Anthony was featured on a one-dollar coin introduced in the United States in 1979. (Ben Klaffke)

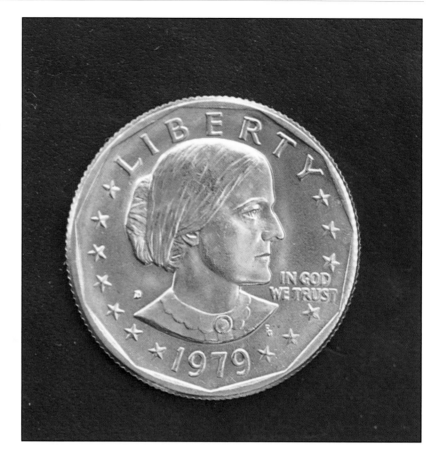

The money people use daily isn't valuable because of the metal or paper used to make it. It is valuable because of what it does for people. It helps people get what they need or want. Money is valuable only because people agree that it is.

CHAPTER 2

How Does It Work?

Cash, checks, and credit cards all allow us to pay for things in different ways.

Paying with Cash

Grandmother might ask you to help her pay cash for groceries. She asks you to count out the cash and hand it to the cashier. The groceries only cost $17.85. You might not have the exact amount the groceries cost. Instead, you might give the cashier more. Maybe you hand over a twenty-dollar bill. The cashier would then give you two one-dollar bills, a dime, and a nickel in change. That adds up to $2.15. The amount you get in change is the amount you paid minus the actual cost of what you bought.

Paying with a Check

What if Grandmother pays for the groceries with a check? She finds a blank check in her checkbook. The check has some information on it. That information includes Grandmother's name and address. The rest of the check is blank because Grandmother hasn't written anything on it yet. Now she fills in the blanks shown on the check. She uses a pen so that no one can erase what she writes and write something else.

When making purchases, people must make the choice between using cash or credit cards.
(PhotoDisc, Inc.)

Grandmother fills in the date, the name of the store, and the amount of the check. She fills in the amount twice, once in numbers and once in words. Grandmother writes very neatly. Someone might still misread her writing. Writing out the amount two different ways makes it less likely for someone to make that mistake.

Grandmother also fills in the "Memo" blank. It reminds her what the check bought. Finally, Grandmother signs the check. She hands it to the cashier.

The cashier may ask Grandmother for identification. Usually, people present a driver's license as identification. The identification shows that the person using the check is the same person who has the account. Checking Grandmother's identification protects her and helps stop crime. Some people steal blank checks so they can use the money in someone else's account.

Identification also assures the store that it will be able to exchange the check for money.

Keeping Track of Checks

Grandmother carefully records the payment in her checkbook. She uses the *check register*. It has places to fill in information about the payment. This information includes the check number. It also

Supermarket cashiers ask for identification when customers write checks to pay for their groceries.
(James L. Shaffer)

includes the date, the name of the store, and the amount of the check. Grandmother will subtract this amount from the number on the far right side of the register. That number is the account balance. It says how much money is left in the account.

This amount is important for Grandmother to know. It tells her she has enough money in the account to cover, or provide for, the check. It is

People must write out the amount of a check twice—once in numbers and once in words. (Ben Klaffke)

also important because of the type of checking
account Grandmother has. Grandmother needs to
have a certain balance to have free checking. If her
account falls below this balance, she will need to
pay a fee for each check she writes. Not all accounts
have free checking. She also may need to pay other
fees, called *service fees*, on her account.

The balance Grandmother needs is fairly high.
The account is a *NOW account*. Grandmother gets
interest on the money she has in the account. Her
bank pays her a certain percentage of her balance.
That percentage is called the interest rate. For
example, suppose Grandmother has a balance of
$3,000. If the interest rate is 3 percent, the amount
of interest is $90. Ninety dollars is 3 percent of
three thousand dollars.

A regular checking account doesn't pay
interest, but the *minimum balance* needed is less.
The minimum balance is the lowest amount
someone can have for free checking and avoid
paying other service fees.

Special accounts don't require a minimum
balance. For these accounts, the account holder
must pay a fee for each check he or she writes.
Grandmother may write many checks in a month.
She might lose money with a special account. With
the NOW account, she can earn money.

How Do Checks Work?

What happens to the check now? How does
it become money for the store? The store has to
endorse the check. It signs or stamps the back of
the check. It then deposits, or puts, the check in
its bank account.

The store's bank must now collect the money
from Grandmother's bank. It sends the check to the
nearest Federal Reserve bank. The Federal Reserve
bank belongs to the Federal Reserve System. This
system is a clearinghouse for checks.

Personal computers allow some people to learn their checking account balances by reading their bank statements from home. (AP/Wide World Photos)

It sorts checks and settles bank accounts. Machines read the computer numbers on the top and bottom of the check. These numbers identify your Grandmother's bank. The system then deducts, or subtracts, the amount of the check from Grandmother's bank. It also credits, or adds, the amount to the store's bank. Then it sends the check on to Grandmother's bank. The check has cleared the system.

Reading a Bank Statement

Grandmother receives her cleared checks with her monthly *bank statement*. This statement records what happened to Grandmother's account within the month. It shows the interest she earned on the account. It also shows any deposits Grandmother made to the account. In addition, it shows her cleared checks. Grandmother can match the bank statement to her check register. She can then know that her record agrees with the bank's. They agree that she hasn't fallen below her minimum balance. They also agree that she has enough money in her account to clear her checks.

Point-of-Sale Cards

Grandmother can use money from her account in another way to buy groceries. She can use a point-of-sale (POS) card. A machine that reads this card is in the checkout line. Grandmother can run the card through the machine. She enters a code on the machine's keys. This code is her personal identification number (PIN). The PIN is secret so that people can't steal money from Grandmother's account. Grandmother also enters the amount of the groceries. She remembers to record the payment

Some gas stations allow people to use point-of-sale cards to pay at the gas pump. (Ben Klaffke)

in her check register. Her POS payments will show on her bank statement along with her check payments.

Paying with a POS card withdraws, or takes, money automatically from Grandmother's account. Writing a check allows money to stay in her account longer. First the store must deposit the check. Then the check must clear the Federal Reserve System. A check usually clears the system in two to three days.

Using a Credit Card

There is a way for Grandmother to wait even longer to pay for the groceries. She can use a credit card. Many checkout lines have machines that read credit cards. Grandmother runs her credit card through this machine. Two receipts print out. Grandmother signs the first one and gives it to the cashier. Her signature says she agreed to the payment. The other receipt Grandmother keeps for her records.

The store got its money when the machine said the payment was approved. The bank or company that gave the credit card to Grandmother paid for the groceries. That bank or company is the issuer of the card. The issuer will send Grandmother a bill for the amount.

The bill comes in the form of a *credit card statement*. A new statement arrives every month. The statement lists all the payments your Grandmother made with the credit card that month. Grandmother can match these payments with her receipts.

The statement also shows the amount Grandmother owes the issuer. It tells when the payment is due. Grandmother doesn't need to pay the total amount she owes right away. She only needs to pay what shows as the minimum payment. That amount may be 2 to 5 percent of

Special machines verify the information contained in the magnetic strip on the back of every credit card. (PhotoDisc, Inc.)

the total. If she doesn't pay the full amount, she will have to pay interest on the unpaid amount.

Credit Limits and Finance Charges

The credit card statement shows the largest amount Grandmother can charge. This amount is her *credit limit*. Alongside it shows the available amount. Grandmother has this amount left to use. It is her credit limit minus the amount she owes.

Grandmother can see the issuer's annual percentage rate (APR) on the statement, too. This is the rate of interest the issuer charges. It can be as high as 21 percent. Grandmother owes the issuer this interest for using its money.

The finance charge on the statement sums up the cost of buying on credit. It shows the cost of interest in dollars. It includes any service fees Grandmother

Many banks offer low introductory annual percentage rates (APRs) to attract new credit card customers.
(James L. Shaffer)

must pay. For example, Grandmother needs to pay
a fee if her payment is late. Different issuers have
different service fees.

Grandmother made sure her issuer didn't charge
a membership fee. She didn't want to pay a fee
simply to have a credit card. She also made sure
the issuer offered a *grace period*. This grace period
allows her not to pay interest. She can pay the full
amount she owes by the due date. Then she
doesn't have to pay the issuer anything more.

Grandmother is able to pay her bill in full each
month. The APR doesn't matter to her. Your Uncle
Leon isn't always able to pay the full amount. He
made sure the issuer of his credit card had a low
APR. That way he doesn't have to pay as much
on his bill.

Cash, checks, credit cards: the same, yet different.
Understanding how each works can help you
decide which to use when.

Where Do You Get It?

You go to Grandmother's bank with her. The two of you walk up to the bank teller standing behind the counter. The bank teller gives Grandmother cash for the checks she endorses.

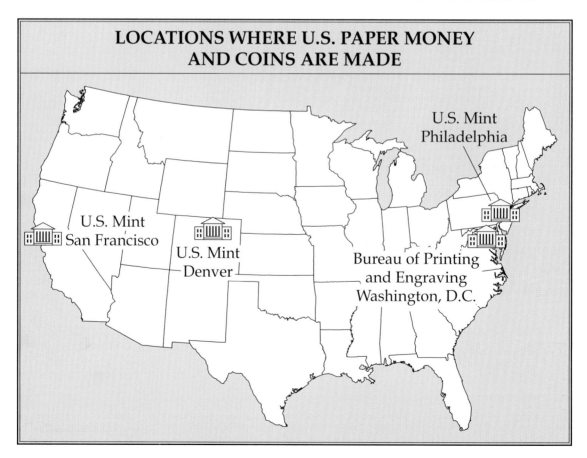

LOCATIONS WHERE U.S. PAPER MONEY AND COINS ARE MADE

U.S. Mint
Philadelphia

U.S. Mint
San Francisco

U.S. Mint
Denver

Bureau of Printing
and Engraving
Washington, D.C.

After serving as Wyoming's first woman governor, Nellie Tayloe Ross was appointed as the first woman to head the U.S. Mint. (Wyoming Division of Cultural Resources)

Where does the bank get the cash? All cash comes from the Department of the Treasury. This part of the government oversees the Bureau of Engraving and Printing and the U.S. *Mint*. The Bureau of Engraving and Printing makes bills. The Mint makes coins.

Making Coins and Printing Money

Three cities have a U.S. Mint. They are Philadelphia, Denver, and San Francisco. The Mint in San Francisco makes only commemorative coins. These coins honor special people or events

NELLIE TAYLOE ROSS (1876-1977)

On May 3, 1933, Nellie Tayloe Ross took command of the United States Mint. She was the first woman ever to head the Mint.

Ross was also the first woman governor of a state. Her husband, William Bradford Ross, was the governor of Wyoming. He died in office. Nellie Tayloe Ross ran for governor in the next election and won.

Ross took office on January 5, 1925. She served one term. Then she gave a series of popular lectures around the country. She spoke in support of the Democratic Party. This activity brought her to the attention of President Franklin Roosevelt. President Roosevelt was a Democrat. He chose Ross to direct the Mint.

This job involved making money for the United States. It also involved overseeing the nation's store of gold and silver. Ross directed the Mint for almost twenty years.

When Ross started, work at the Mint was done by hand. The work went very slowly. Ross decided it was time to use machines to do some of the work. She offered awards for ideas from her employees. Two employees won an award for inventing one particular machine. This machine stamped a design on coins twice as quickly as before.

Ross improved the Mint still more. The Mint had branches in three cities: Philadelphia, Denver, and San Francisco. Each branch had its own system for doing things. Ross brought all the branches under one system. The Mint then ran in a more orderly way.

The changes Ross made in the Mint reduced its costs. In 1950, she gave Congress back $1 million. The Congress had given her $4.8 million to run the Mint. She hadn't needed it all.

Ross lived to be one hundred and one years old. She died on December 19, 1977. She had been born on November 29, 1876.

in American history. Under the direction of Nellie Tayloe Ross in the 1930's and 1940's, the U.S. Mint also minted coins for many foreign governments. The word "mint" means to make a coin out of metal.

The Coinage Act of 1965 changed the metal content of U.S. quarters and dimes from pure silver to a combination of silver and copper. This combination, known as an *alloy*, allowed the U.S. Mint to make coins more cheaply without changing the face value or worth of the coins.

The Bureau of Engraving and Printing is in Washington, D.C. Look closely at a bill. You see many swirling lines. It is hard to copy the engravings that made these lines. It is important that bills are difficult to copy. Fake bills spoil people's trust in their money. People will try to use the fake bills, but they are worthless.

People who make fake bills are counterfeiters. Counterfeiters are criminals. The U.S. Secret Service began to help fight counterfeiting during the Civil War. As much as one-third of the U.S. bills used then were *counterfeit*. The Secret Service is part of the Treasury Department.

Spotting a Counterfeit

The Secret Service can detect counterfeit bills. Real bills have a secret formula ink. Also,

In 1996, the Treasury Department introduced new hundred-dollar bills that have been designed to discourage counterfeiting. (AP/Wide World Photos)

the paper in bills is a secret blend of cotton and linen fibers. This paper is special in another way. There are color threads in it that won't photocopy. In 1996, the Treasury Department issued a new hundred-dollar bill. Its color threads glow red in ultraviolet light. Plans are for all denominations above one dollar to have these color threads.

Counterfeit coins are less of a problem than counterfeit bills. It probably costs more than the coin's face value to make a counterfeit coin. Some people try to use counterfeit coins in vending machines. Most of these vending machines have devices to detect counterfeit coins. These devices measure the weight, diameter, and thickness of the coins placed in the machine against the known measurements of legal coins.

Getting Cash

Sometimes Grandmother doesn't go to the bank teller to get cash. Sometimes she uses an automated teller machine (ATM). Most ATMs pay out cash in $20 bills only. Grandmother must go to the teller inside the bank if she wants other denominations of bills or if she wants change.

Grandmother got the card she uses at the ATM from her bank. ATM machines can be found inside grocery stores. They are at airports, too. Grandmother can use her ATM card to buy more things than cash. At some ATM machines she can buy stamps. She can also use her ATM card to make point-of-sale (POS) purchases. She can make POS purchases at the gas station and the grocery store, for example.

Traveler's Checks and Personal Checks

Once, Grandmother bought *traveler's checks* from the bank before leaving on a trip. She can use these checks all over the world. They are safer than cash.

They aren't money until Grandmother signs them twice. She signed the checks when she bought them. She must sign them again when she uses them.

Grandmother buys personal checks from her bank, too. These are the checks she has in her checkbook. Uncle Leon buys personal checks from a company through the mail. He can choose from many different designs for his checks. The company promises not to give out the personal information on the check.

Applying for a Credit Card

Grandmother's credit card is from her bank. She applied at the bank for the card. The application asked for certain information. It asked Grandmother's income. It asked how long she had lived at her present address. It asked her to list her bank accounts and her other credit cards. Her answers scored points. For example, the higher her income, the more points she scored. Grandmother's score added up to her *credit rating*. Her credit rating shows that the bank can count on her to pay what she owes.

Uncle Leon doesn't have a very good credit rating. He recently graduated from college. He has never lived anywhere longer than six months. He has never had a credit card. He is also paying off college loans. Uncle Leon applied for a secured card from the bank. The secured card looks like a credit card. It allows Uncle Leon to charge up to a certain amount. He must have at least that amount in his bank account. His bank account secures, or backs with money, what Uncle Leon buys on the card.

Some department stores and chain stores offer their own credit cards. Only that store takes them. Gas companies also offer credit cards that can be used only at their stations.

KENNETH I. CHENAULT (1951-   )

"You're equal to the task." Kenneth I. Chenault remembers hearing these words often from his father. Chenault is an African American. His father, Hortenius, was a successful dentist. Hortenius Chenault fought prejudice. He succeeded against barriers put in his way.

Kenneth Chenault showed his ability to succeed early. He was president of his high school class. After graduating from college, he went to Harvard Law School. Harvard is one of the best schools in the country.

In 1981, Chenault accepted a job at American Express. He started with the part of the company that sells high-quality goods. These goods included luggage and computers. Three years later, Chenault headed this business. Sales increased 5 percent a year. By 1989, he was president of the company's charge card business in the United States. After being named vice chairman of the American Express Company in 1995, Chenault began exploring ways to encourage banks to issue American Express cards to consumers and business customers.

Satisfied customers are important to Chenault. Chenault added to the businesses that accept American Express cards. He knew that people with cards liked to use them everywhere. He also knew that people want good service. They like having a personal representative with the company. Customers can always talk to that representative when they have questions.

Credit Cards and Charge Cards

Most banks offer Visa and MasterCard credit cards. Some private companies offer other credit cards. Sears offers the Discover card, and American Express offers an Optima credit card. American Express also offers charge cards. Members can charge purchases on these cards, but they must pay their monthly bill in full. It is harder to get a charge card than a credit card. You must prove that you can pay off your charges every month. Other companies that offer charge cards include Diners Club and Carte Blanche.

It is also hard to get a premium credit card. These are called "gold" and "platinum" cards. Fees are higher for these cards than those charged for regular credit cards. Credit limits are higher, too. Special services come with these cards. Many gold and platinum cards offer special travel services.

Banks and Credit Unions

Grandmother's bank is a commercial bank. Most banks are commercial banks. They are called "commercial" because they only had businesses as customers when they began.

Aunt Sylvia banks at a credit union. A credit union is like a club where members have accounts. People at the company where Aunt Sylvia works belong to the same credit union. Aunt Sylvia has a checking account and a credit card with her credit union. Her fees are lower than Grandmother's. Most people at the credit union know one another. They are less likely to default, or not pay what they owe, on what they borrow from the credit union. Therefore, the credit union doesn't have to pay high fees to cover the cost of customers who default.

Money certainly doesn't grow on trees. It comes from the government, banks, credit unions, and private companies, too.

What Are the Rules?

"Prices keep going up!" Grandmother says at the grocery store. "A dollar use to buy more when I was your age!"

Uncle Leon studied economics in college. He explains that economics has a law of supply and demand. This law says that the more of something there is, the less value it has. So, the more money there is in the economy, the less the money is worth. Therefore, the less it can buy. It has less buying power.

Inflation and Depression

Inflation happens when money loses its buying power. People may have more money, but it doesn't seem to buy much. People feel that they are paying more for less.

An economic *depression* happens when income and consumer spending drop to very low levels. Money is very hard to get. Prices fall, but people are afraid they won't have enough money to buy what they need to live.

In the years before 1900, the United States economy had many depressions. Part of the problem was how far money had to travel from bank to bank. It took banks a long time

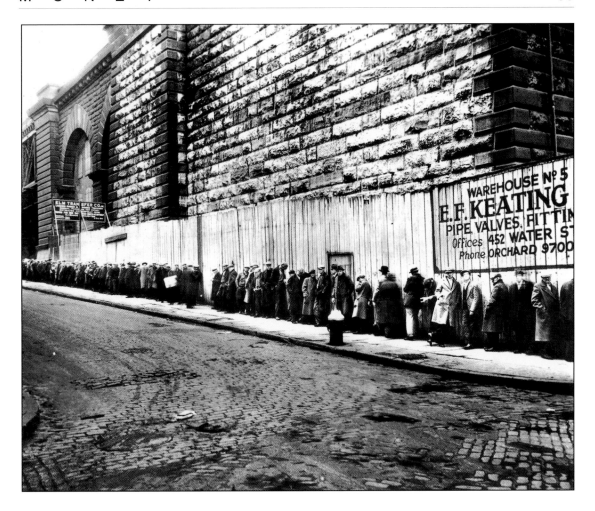

to cash checks. People suspected that the banks had no money. They hurried to withdraw their money before the banks closed. The banks quickly ran out of cash and then had to close. Businesses that borrowed from the banks also closed. People lost jobs. The country fell into a depression.

During the Great Depression of the 1930's, many banks and businesses failed and millions of people lost their jobs.
(Library of Congress)

Controlling the Nation's Money Supply

The United States Congress had a solution for economic depressions. In 1913, it created the Federal Reserve System, known as "the Fed." The Constitution gives Congress the power to make money and control its value. Congress passed its power to control money's value on to the Fed. The Fed does this by controlling the money flow, or how much money is in the economy.

The Fed controls the money flow by being a central bank. It acts as a clearinghouse for checks. It makes sure money moves from bank to bank without delay. The Fed also sets the interest rates banks charge. People pay interest on the money they borrow. The higher the interest rate, the more interest people pay. They borrow less and they spend less, too. Less money is in the economy. The Fed raises interest rates to slow inflation.

To help the economy grow, the Fed may lower interest rates. People borrow more money. They also spend more. More money is available. More jobs are, too.

If inflation starts, the Fed raises interest rates again. The Fed helps the economy stay healthy enough to grow. It also slows growth to keep people safe from inflation.

Another way the Fed controls money flow is by regulating how much money banks must keep in reserve. A bank's reserve is the cash it has ready to give to customers. The more money a bank has in reserve, the less it has to loan. The Fed increases reserves to stop inflation. It lowers reserves to put more money into the economy and help it grow.

Insuring People's Deposits

Grandmother made sure she had an account with a bank belonging to the Federal Deposit Insurance Corporation (FDIC). Then if the bank closed, she wouldn't lose all the money she kept there. The FDIC would pay her up to $100,000 on her account. The FDIC also would pay if the bank lost her money in a fire or robbery.

The FDIC started during the Great Depression of the 1930's. Many banks closed. People who had money deposited with those banks lost it. In 1933,

the government passed the Banking Act. This law created the FDIC. People could have confidence their money would be safe in banks belonging to the FDIC.

The sign in this bank's front window identifies it as a member of the Federal Insurance Deposit Corporation (FDIC). (Ben Klaffke)

Obeying the Rules

The Federal Reserve System also makes sure banks follow banking laws. For example, people younger than eighteen can't open a checking account. The law calls people below age eighteen "minors." A check is a legal contract. A contract binds people to its terms. Contracts can't bind minors. Therefore, a minor's signature on a check doesn't guarantee someone can cash it.

Minors can have joint checking accounts with adults. For example, you and your father may have a joint checking account. Both of your names are on the checks. When you want to write checks, your father must also sign them before anyone can exchange the checks for cash.

Many people feel more comfortable about their finances when they have overdraft protection on their checking accounts. (Jim Whitmer)

Checking accounts have other rules. Cousin Jesse had to pay the bank a fee for a *bounced check*. He didn't have enough money in his account to pay the check. The store he made the check out to couldn't cash it. The check "bounced" back to Cousin Jesse. He called it a "rubber check."

Some banks have added other rules that apply to their customers who have checking and savings accounts. These banks are finding it expensive to keep many small branch offices open and safe for their customers. It is cheaper for banks to let customers use automated teller machines instead. To help pay the salaries of tellers and security guards, some banks have begun charging fees to those customers who come inside the bank to deposit, transfer, or withdraw money.

Safety and Protection

Grandmother has overdraft checking. "Overdraft" is another name for a bounced check. The bank pays any overdraft Grandmother might have. It lends her the money to cover the check. She doesn't have to pay a fee for the check. She does have to pay a fee for having overdraft checking. She is willing to pay that fee. A bounced check could lower her credit rating. Grandmother's good credit rating is important to her. It helps her to buy on credit when she needs to.

In 1969, Congress passed the Truth in Lending Act. This law protects you when you use credit. It says the creditor must put the terms of credit in writing. These terms include the finance charge and the APR.

All credit cards give you sixty days to dispute, or argue against, charges on your bill. Once Grandmother found the same charge listed twice on her bill. She reported the error in writing. She didn't have to pay the charge in dispute that month. She did have to pay the rest of the bill.

Some banks have begun charging customers additional fees for the convenience of using tellers inside branch offices.
(Ben Klaffke)

The law gives your creditor the right to get money from you when you don't pay your bills. For example, the issuer of your credit card can take money out of your salary. Like checks, credit card agreements don't legally apply to minors. An adult must co-sign a minor's card. That adult accepts responsibility for payment.

Each state has its own laws about credit cards. Uncle Leon lives in California and has a credit card from a bank in Arizona. The laws that apply to his credit card are Arizona's laws.

Laws about money, checks, and credit cards exist to make sure people use them safely and responsibly. These laws protect both creditors and borrowers. They protect us all.

What Does It Mean to Me?

I get a weekly allowance. I know I only have that amount of money to buy things each week. I have to make choices about what I buy. I like making choices. It makes me feel grown up. I am learning what is important to me. Playing pinball is important to me. I spend any extra money I have on pinball. The pinball machine only takes coins. I always make sure I have coins with me.

Most pinball machines need coins in order to work. (James L. Shaffer)

Other Money Options

Grandmother mostly uses coins to make calls on pay phones. She uses a card, though, to make long distance calls. Long distance calls require many coins. Using the card is easier. It is a prepaid card. Grandmother already paid for the calls when she bought the card. Each call she makes subtracts from the amount she paid for the card. For example, she paid five dollars for the card. We made a long distance call to Aunt Paula to say when we would meet her at the airport. After the call, Grandmother had three dollars less on the card.

Aunt Paula uses a prepaid card to make calls and ride the subway, too. She often uses cards to pay for things. Aunt Paula doesn't like what she calls "paperwork." She says writing checks and recording them on a check register wastes paper. She says it wastes time, too.

Making Money Stretch

Aunt Paula especially likes using her credit cards. She can use what she buys before she has to pay for it. She also can use her money longer— until she has to pay her bill. She can stretch her budget more. She feels every credit card she has is a bargain. She is also aware that someday she must pay for everything on her credit cards.

Aunt Paula makes good use of the grace period on her credit cards. She tries to pay her bills in full each month. When she can't pay in full, she sends in as much as she can. The minimum payment is the lowest amount she can send. She can always send more. The more she sends, the less she owes. The less she owes, the less interest she pays on her next bill. Aunt Paula tries not to pay very much interest. That way she avoids paying a big cost for buying on credit.

Convenience and Safety

Aunt Paula also likes knowing she can use her credit cards all over the country. Aunt Paula travels often. Most hotels and restaurants don't take out-of-state checks. A personal check with an address in another state is an out-of-state check. Many hotels and restaurants take credit cards,

By reducing the need for large amounts of cash, credit cards make shopping safer for customers and for the stores where they shop. **(Jim Whitmer)**

though. Aunt Paula also can use her store credit cards at any branch of that store.

Aunt Paula likes other advantages that come with using credit cards. If she has a problem with something she buys, she doesn't have to pay for it when her bill comes. She can wait until she resolves the problem. Once an airline canceled her flight after she had paid for her ticket with a credit card. She didn't have to pay the amount of the ticket on her bill until the airline rescheduled the flight. If she had paid by check, she would have had to stop payment on the check. Her bank would have charged a fee for that service.

Another reason Aunt Paula likes using credit cards is she doesn't feel safe carrying a lot of cash. Neither does Grandmother. Grandmother agrees that cash is too easy to lose and can easily be stolen. She prefers using checks. Grandmother knows when she buys something with a check exactly how much less she has in her account. She subtracts the amount of the check on her check register. She knows when she falls below her balance and will have to pay service fees. She knows what those fees are, too. For example, the fee to use her ATM card is one dollar a month. Grandmother says she likes knowing exactly where her money goes.

Grandmother is on a fixed income. She has only a certain amount of money to live on each month. She doesn't want to think about making different payments each month on her credit card. She also doesn't want to think about interest adding on to what she owes on the card.

Avoiding Credit Card Fraud

Grandmother worries about credit card fraud, too. Credit card fraud has to do with counterfeit, or fake, cards. Criminals get account numbers and names by stealing credit cards or credit card

receipts. They sometimes get account information by tapping into computer files. Then they make new magnetic strips that include this information. They attach these strips to existing credit cards they have stolen or to blank credit cards they have stolen or copied.

Aunt Paula reminds Grandmother that she doesn't have to pay more than fifty dollars on charges when someone steals her credit card. Grandmother answers that she ends up paying more than that. Stores raise prices, and banks and

To prevent credit card fraud, stores compare the customer's signature with the signature that appears on the back of the credit card.
(James L. Shaffer)

credit card companies charge high interest rates to make up the money they lose on credit card fraud.

Aunt Paula says it is important to have choices on how to pay for things. She says people have different needs at different times in their lives. She reminds Grandmother how Uncle Leon was able to buy things for his new baby on credit. He could not have bought them otherwise. She also tells Grandmother how credit card companies use technology to stay one step ahead of counterfeiters. For example, credit card companies are making harder-to-copy codes on magnetic strips.

Grandmother says it is time to stop talking and start eating. I agree. Aunt Paula wants to take us all out to dinner. She says she is too hungry to stop by the ATM machine and get cash. She says she will put the dinner on her credit card. Everyone is glad Aunt Paula has the credit card.

Glossary

bank statement: a report the bank sends every month. The report shows deposits, withdrawals, and services fees on an account for that month.

barter: a way of trading without using money.

bill: paper money; also, a statement of what someone owes.

bounced check: a check that someone can't exchange for money. It returns, or bounces back, to the check writer.

cash: bills, change, or a combination of both; also, to exchange a check for money.

change: coin money; also, the money you get back when you pay more than something costs.

check register: a list of the checks someone writes. It also shows the balance on the account.

checking account: a bank account that lets a person write a check. This check draws on the money the person has in the account.

credit card: a plastic card issued by a bank (bankcard) or other lender that allows you to purchase items and pay for them later. Sometimes called a *charge card*.

credit card statement: a monthly bill from the issuer of the credit card.

credit limit: the largest amount someone can borrow.

credit rating: a score showing someone's ability to pay on credit.

counterfeit: fake money that criminals make and try to pass off as real.

currency: the money that a country uses.

denomination: the amount a piece of currency is worth. It is usually in writing on the currency.

depression: a time when money is hard to get. People lose jobs and don't spend much during a depression.

endorse: to sign or stamp a check so that you can exchange it for money.

face value: the amount a bill or coin can buy.

grace period: the time a credit card user has to pay a bill in full and not pay interest.

inflation: a time when a lot of money is in use. The money loses its value and prices rise.

interest: the amount of money you pay in addition to the amount you borrowed; also, the cost of borrowing.

legal tender: money that the law says is acceptable as payment.

medium of exchange: something people accept as valuable. People use it to trade for something they want or need.

minimum balance: the lowest amount someone can have for free checking.

mint: to make coins; also, a factory that makes coins.

NOW account: a checking account that earns interest.

point-of-sale (POS) card: a small plastic card that automatically takes money from a checking account.

rate of exchange: the amount money costs in another currency.

service fee: a fee for extra work a bank or creditor does on an account. Service fees include late fees on credit cards and stop payment fees on checking accounts.

traveler's checks: special checks that people use as money all over the world.

Sources

Adler, David A. *All Kinds of Money*. New York: Franklin Watts, 1984. (3rd-4th grade)

Adler, David A. *Inflation: When Prices Go Up, Up, Up*. New York: Franklin Watts, 1985. (3rd-4th grade)

Briers, Audrey. *Money*. New York: Bookwright Press, 1987. (4th-6th grade)

Cantwell, Lois. *Money and Banking*. New York: Franklin Watts, 1984. (7th-8th grade)

Cribb, Joe. *Money*. Eyewitness Books. New York: Alfred A. Knopf, 1990. (7th-8th grade)

Fodor, R.V. *Nickels, Dimes, and Dollars*. New York: William Morrow, 1980. (7th-8th grade)

Maestro, Betsy. *The Story of Money*. New York: Clarion Books, 1993. (4th-6th grade)

Spies, Karen Bornemann. *Our Money*. Brookfield, Conn.: Millbrook Press, 1992. (5th-7th grade)

Wallace, G. David. *Money Basics*. Englewood Cliffs, N.J.: Prentice-Hall, 1984. (6th-8th grade)

Index